Israel

ISRAEL LAND OF PROMISE

PHOTOGRAPHY BY DAVID FITZGERALD

TEXT BY RICHARD E. ROBY AND CATHY A. KASS, Ed.D

EDITORIAL CONSULTANT, R. MEIR ROBY

GRAPHIC ARTS CENTER PUBLISHING COMPANY, PORTLAND, OREGON

International Standard Book Number 0-932575-92-7
Library of Congress Catalog Number 88-80542
© MCMLXXXVIII by Graphic Arts Center Publishing Company
P.O. Box 10306 • Portland, Oregon 97210 • 503/226-2402
Editor-in-Chief • Douglas A. Pfeiffer
Associate Editor • Jean Andrews
Designer • Robert Reynolds
Cartographer • Tom Patterson and Manoa Mapworks
Typographer • Paul O. Giesey/Adcrafters
Color Separations • Color Graphics
Printer • Dynagraphics, Inc.
Bindery • Lincoln & Allen
Printed in the United States of America

To Helen . . .
who instilled in me the love of travel
and the wonders of adventure.

DAVID FITZGERALD

To our parents . . .
who helped us discover the magic of
dreaming—and to Nonnie and to all those
who have dreamed of seeing the Land of
Promise but did not.

RICHARD E. ROBY AND CATHY A. KASS, ED.D.

The photographer and authors of ISRAEL: LAND OF PROMISE
acknowledge with deep gratitude the support and assistance
from each of the following: Troy and Dollie Smith, for catching
the vision and enabling us to produce this work through their
financial support and encouragement; Israel Ministry of Tourism,
for direction and information; Avner and Shoshana Kahanov, for
helping us see the real Israel through the eyes of those who have
always called it home; Elie Saada, for escorting the authors
throughout Israel and patiently answering questions with continued
enthusiasm; Sandy Lee, for taking untold hours of personal time to
type and retype the manuscripts and related correspondence; Brenda
Hays, for her remarkable editing skills; and Rabbi David A. Packman,
Temple B'nai Israel, Oklahoma City, for his valuable assistance.

■ *Half-title:* Devout Jews believe those buried on the Mount of Olives will
reenter Jerusalem first on Judgment Day. ■ *Frontispiece:* At Massada, 967
men, women, and children chose suicide rather than become captive to the
Romans. ■ *Right:* "Depart, go up hence, thou and the people that thou hast
brought up out of the land of Egypt, unto the land of which I swore unto
Abraham, to Isaac, and to Jacob." Exodus 33:1

*All scriptures used in this book are from the Holy Scriptures according to the Masoretic Text, the Jewish
Publication Society of America, Philadelphia, Copyright 1917, 1945.*

■ *Above:* Originally Mount Moriah, the Temple Mount—important to Jews, Christians, and Moslems alike—is the site of the Dome of the Rock. ■ *Right:* Within the sixteenth-century Turkish walls are four distinct sections of the Old City—the Jewish, Christian, Arab, and Armenian quarters. ■ *Overleaf:* The Dome of the Rock, located in the Temple Square, is considered by Moslems to be at the exact center of the world.

■ *Left:* In the late 1800s, Russia's Alexander III established the Church of Mary Magdalene near the Garden of Gethsemane. ■ *Above:* The Old City of Jerusalem (or the City of David) grew and was given a different look when David's son, Solomon, expanded the city some three thousand years ago.

■ *Above:* Mount Zion, once an important key to the security of Jerusalem and a natural defense against the Romans, is recognized as the symbolic site of King David's tomb. It is said that Jesus observed Passover with his disciples on Mount Zion above the tomb. ■ *Right:* Twice destroyed—once in 614 A.D. by the Persians and again in 1009 by the Caliph El Hakim—the Church of the Holy Sepulchre still reflects much of its original architecture.

■ *Left:* The Church of the Holy Sepulchre, although the center of controversy about the authenticity of its location, is still considered by many to have been erected over the tomb where Jesus was buried. ■ *Above:* A teenager becomes a man during a Bar Mitzvah ceremony at The Western Wall. Many Israelis, as well as foreign pilgrims, make the trek to Jerusalem and The Wall to add special significance to this traditional rite of passage.

Praying at the Wall is a deeply religious experience for today's Jew.

THE LAND OF PROMISE

Today's travelers to Israel find themselves weaving in and out of ancient biblical history. Just as Jews and Arabs coexist amid an often tense, sometimes volatile atmosphere, so does history meet head-on with a more contemporary Israel.

Pick a region, town, or city — any city — and, sometimes, under the layers of sand, dust, and time one may uncover the true picture of the stuff from which this land is made. The careful eye may catch a rare glimpse of the Israel that is far beyond the tourist attractions and the often-visited historical and biblical sites.

Perhaps it is the monotone drabness of the desert, bleached of all color by the tears of literally millions of souls, that makes the most dramatic impression. It is in the desert where one can still find the remnants of past civilizations jutting out of nowhere — Roman "highways" and an occasional column or architectural ruin. Beyond all else, the ultimate mercy of the land is evidenced by that which *remains*.

While most Western nations date their cultures in a few centuries, Israel's history is made up of countless centuries. Ruled by a multitude of governments — both good and bad — each seems to have left some impression or custom never to be forgotten, but instead incorporated into a land unique among all others.

One must look beyond the desert and biblical Jerusalem to get a true picture of Israel. As beautiful and significant as Jerusalem is to Israel, the constant reminder must be that Jerusalem is not all of Israel. Limited perhaps by time and energy, but more often because of a lack of knowledge of the land and its people, pilgrims tend to see and visit only a minute part of Israel.

It is, perhaps, this more accurate picture that brings into focus the reasons the land continues to be one of open hostility and bloodshed — generation after generation of war between neighbors.

Perhaps it is this "feeling," the feeling of conquering lest one be conquered, that pits neighbor against neighbor. And perhaps herein lies the genesis of the Israeli personality — sometimes abrupt, often defensive, and occasionally even cynical. In contrast, nowhere on earth can one find a people with such a zest for life and a willingness to laugh at themselves.

Israel is a focal point for at least three different religions, and such a merging of faiths in a single country tends to generate tension rather than peace. Wracked by centuries of war, occupation, and — oftentimes — senseless bloodshed, Israel survives in spite of those who have sought to undermine her destiny.

"Hear the voice of my supplications, when I cry unto thee..."   Psalm 28:2

As beautiful as she is, Israel projects a sense of paranoia with regard to everything about her—her people, her business, and her government. The fragile joy of independence is so fresh in the minds of Israelis that there seems always to be a spirit of defensiveness in the people who have yearned so long for peace, lest freedom slip from their grasp yet again.

Reality is that within the land of Moses and his followers—in the land where Jesus lived, taught, and died at the hands of the Romans—is a large contingent of people who neither profess any religious beliefs nor practice any religion, either privately or openly.

Thus, out of the many cultures which contrast as starkly as the land itself emerges the Israel of today: Israel! Land of Promise.

THE TAPESTRY

Woven into the ever-changing tapestry of a complex country, inevitably bound for further testing of will and strength, is a people bent on survival.

Tested by time yet living in a young country new-born only in 1948, the people of Israel are relatively small in number but large in the strength of their commitment to the building of a single nation from this unique mixture of cultures that is Israel today.

To understand the people who call Israel home, one must be aware of their history. Following the destruction of the Second Temple, the first-century Jews were conquered by invading nations, driven from their home-land, and dispersed to all corners of the world. During this period, commonly known as the Diaspora, the land now called Israel was ruled first by the Romans, followed in succession by the Persians, Arabs, Crusaders, Turks, and the British. Over the centuries, while Jews lived in varying numbers throughout the world and contributed to the civilization of many nations alongside their countrymen, nevertheless, they were subject to prejudice and persecution in every country they inhabited.

In their search for freedom, Jews began returning in the late 1800s to the land "promised" centuries ago. The waves of immigration brought a mixture of cultures and customs, a people bound together only by their belief in Judaism. They ranged from the Ashkenazim, the Yiddish-speaking people from Central and Eastern Europe, to the Sephardim, the descendants of Jews forced from their homes during the Spanish Inquisition and who survived under limited protection in the Moslem East.

Conservative estimates are that over 60 percent of all Jewish Israelis can trace their recent heritage to the Middle East. They have emigrated from countries in Africa, such as Morocco and Ethiopia, as well as from Iraq, Iran, Turkey, Egypt, and Yemen.

Another wave of immigration began in 1950, with immigrants arriving from Arabic-speaking countries, followed more recently by Ethiopian Jews escaping famine and starvation.

During the centuries that Jews all over the world struggled for survival, Palestinian Arabs and Bedouins were living in a land called Palestine. The Bedouins roamed the land, as their nomadic ancestors had done, scarcely concerned with or affected by the politics of governments. The Arabs, however, lived mostly in small villages and attempted to adapt to the ruling powers. Over the years, some Arabs organized into political entities called Jordan, Syria, Saudi Arabia, Lebanon, and Iraq.

During the nearly three decades of British rule, a spirit of nationalism grew in the Arab community as well as among the Jews, rekindling the ancient hatreds as they competed for the same small piece of land each believed to be rightfully theirs. These tensions continue today, in spite of the fact that Arabs and Jews live and work side by side. In recent years, the greatest stresses have been between Israel and two groups: neighboring Arabs who deny Israel's right to exist and Palestinian Arabs who live in the occupied areas known as the West Bank and the Gaza Strip.

Approximately one-fifth of the population of Israel (excluding the occupied territories) is comprised of non-Jews, with the Arab Moslems making up the largest such group. A number of Christians also live in Israel, mostly Roman Catholic and Greek Orthodox. Less-known and in even smaller numbers are the Druze, a religion with origins dating back only about a thousand years — a relatively short time by Jewish standards. Others who have found a home in the "promised land" include Circassians (Moslems from the Caucasus Mountains) and the Bahais.

Depending upon the perspective, the word "peace" means different things to different people. The Arab often seems to coexist *in spite of* the Jew, feeling keenly the loss of a time which meant prosperity and control instead of what many Arabs consider mere existence today.

Under tenuous terms of peace, at best, the Jew, the Christian, and the Arab do somehow live together in this country of four million people. Yet, it is the *Sabra,* the native-born Israeli, who is emerging as the true sociological reflection of today's Israel. *Sabras* now make up the majority of the nation's population.

Just as its architecture reflects the combined layers of civilization that form the "body" of Israel, so, too, do its people reflect the layers of customs, acquired during the Diaspora, that form the "soul" of the country.

Each group of immigrants brought its own customs, language, and ideas, including variations of Judaic practices. Yet they came together with one purpose: to build a nation — their "promised land" — a nation that would

A sealed entrance to the Chapel of the Ascension is an Arab's welcome refuge.

In the Arab Quarter of the Old City, a minaret, or prayer tower, is overshadowed by television antennas.

offer freedom for themselves and their children. A strong, determined spirit, molded from their memories of the past, has made the modern Israeli worthy of being called *Sabra,* a word taken from the name for a cactus fruit which is hard and prickly on the outside, and soft and sweet on the inside.

After years of strife and persecution, the Israelis are a determined people who refuse to be denied their land.

The contrasts in the tapestry woven to comprise the State of Israel are obvious. Differences in the nation's culture, language, religion, land forms, education, and even in her political philosophy are so evident one wonders how a country like this could be so prosperous and successful.

Israel's cities — both archeological and historical wonders — are a modern phenomenon as well. Productive farm communities thrive within a stone's throw of cosmopolitan cities. Fields and orchards of healthy, green crops seem to spring from barren sand and rock. To the north lies the busy, thriving Sea of Galilee, while to the south is the salty Dead Sea.

Diversity is also obvious in the economy, which ranges from the main industries of tourism and cut diamonds to a wide variety of agricultural products such as citrus fruits, sunflowers, barley and olives. The markets and shopping areas include the hectic stalls located in the narrow streets of the Arab Quarter to the elegant shops of the rebuilt Roman Cardo in the Jewish section of Jerusalem.

Eretz Yisrael, the land of Israel, is on the eastern Mediterranean Coast. Established by resolution of the United Nations following World War II, this country of slightly more than 8,000 square miles won its independence as a homeland for the Jewish people in spite of cries from the neighboring Arab countries.

By the hundreds, men, women, and children renounced other homelands and gave up established lives to risk everything in Israel in order to "teach" the land how to grow. They came from many countries to a land barren except for its history and the love and devotion of its people.

In a land steeped in tradition and rivalry, there seemed little likelihood of teaching anything to grow—except conflict. As the religious—and the not-so-religious—gathered to create a new land, oftentimes there seemed little reason to hope. But with strong perseverance and determination, these pioneers built communal settlements called *kibbutzim* and forced the land to produce. All they had to offer was sacrifice, hard work, and commitment to their traditions and history as well as their belief in the future.

Even the land itself is one of contrasts. From rugged mountain areas to sprawling valleys and plains, the country appears to be carved out of rock and wind-swept sands. Lush, green plains now occupy an area that once was the barren, sandy home of Bedouin tribes who roamed the countryside tending their flocks. The miracle of transformation was not a miracle in and of itself—it was a miracle of hard work rendered by the faithful workers of the *kibbutzim.*

Many died developing this land — some from sheer overwork, while others lost their lives at the hands of those who believed the land to be rightfully theirs for centuries. The *kibbutzim* were often attacked by some of their neighbors who resented their presence.

Today, the fruits of those early labors are legendary. From 1909 when Degania, the very first *kibbutz,* was founded on the shores of the Sea of Galilee to today, the number of active *kibbutzim* has grown to approximately two hundred. Several generations of workers have changed the landscape into fertile, productive farmlands.

While only 4 percent of Israel's population lives on the *kibbutz,* the contributions of these workers to the development of Israel were extremely significant. Indeed, their support of the nation's economy continues, not only in the area of agriculture but also in manufacturing and tourism. Self-contained communities, the *kibbutzim* offer their members food, housing, and education, as well as medical care and clothing. All members receive a small allowance for personal expenses and a place to live for the rest of their lives.

Although life on a *kibbutz* has a special fascination for many, more common is the life-style found on a *moshav.* In these agricultural villages, families live in their own homes, and in some instances also work their own plots of land. Often, however, the land is worked communally.

The energy of the workers of the *kibbutzim* and *moshavim* helped build the land of Israel — economically to be sure — but also spiritually. Their commitment to their tasks and their zest for life has become an important part of the Israeli psyche.

If Israel's land comprises its body and the people its soul, then surely Jerusalem is the country's heart!

Since the days of David, Jerusalem has been the center of the world for many. It is Jerusalem that all three of the world's monotheistic religions, in their respective ways, revere as a holy city. The Temple Mount is a location considered holy by Moslems, Jews, and Christians alike.

"Next year in Jerusalem," the last words of the traditional Passover Seder, or meal, is repeated by Jews today just as it has been for centuries. The Temple Mount of Jerusalem is where the Second Temple was built on the same site where the First Temple stood before its destruction. The Western, or Wailing, Wall is the only remnant of what were once the walls surrounding Temple Mount. The Wailing Wall received its name because of the anguish expressed over the destruction of the Temple.

Arabic newspapers attest to the multilingual and ethnic mix of the country.

Religious pilgrims retrace Jesus' last steps, known as the Stations of the Cross.

For Arabs, Jerusalem is the most sacred of places, second only to Mecca and Medina. The Dome of the Rock is considered one of the most important monuments of the Islamic religion because it covers the Moriah Rock, believed to be Mohammed's point of ascension into the heavens.

Christians hold Jerusalem sacred as the site of Jesus' presentation as a baby and where he came as a twelve-year-old boy to discuss theological matters with the scribes. Here, too, according to Matthew, Jesus came to chase away the money changers from the Temple.

Also in Jerusalem—not far from Bethlehem, the birthplace of Jesus—are the areas where Jesus lived and died. The Mount of Olives overlooks the city, and within the walls of the Old City is the *Via Dolorosa,* the Street of Sorrows, with the fourteen Stations of the Cross, which Jesus walked on the way to His crucifixion.

Since Israel's "birth" in 1948, Jerusalem has been divided in two—half occupied by Jordan and half by Israel—per the United Nations resolution.

For the first twenty years, Jews were prohibited from crossing the border to visit the Western Wall, but after the Six-Day War in 1967, the city was reunited, and the Western Wall again became accessible.

Juxtaposed beside the magnetism of the Old City of Jerusalem with its holy and historical sites, the "other" Jerusalem is a modern, vibrant city filled with fascinating neighborhoods, respected museums, and elegant shops. It is the center of government and the home of the *Knesset,* the Israeli parliament. Jerusalem is home to numerous educational institutions, ranging from the traditional *yeshiva* to the most modern university. Here, also, are some of the finest medical facilities in the world.

Other cities which contribute significantly to the country are Haifa and Tel Aviv, both located on the Mediterranean. Haifa, Israel's major seaport, is connected by shipping routes with the rest of the Mediterranean. It is uniquely built on three different levels—the lowest being the Old City of Haifa which adjoins the harbor and coastal strip. The middle and upper levels are connected by a modern funicular railway system.

Claimed by many to be Israel's most beautiful city, Haifa — also a bustling center of business and commerce — is home to the country's largest industrial area. In fact, in Haifa, one can find tremendous energy sources other than its large oil refinery. Its residents are known for their hard work, thus earning for their city the title "Workers' City" as testimony to the rigorous life-style of those living in Haifa.

Partially built on the side of Mt. Carmel, Haifa was discussed as a possible defense position against the German Army in 1942. While the "Carmel Plan" was never activated, the enduring spirit of the Israeli people still prevails in those who call Haifa home.

With its many museums and art galleries, Haifa seems to be at the center of the country's educational and cultural experience. It is there that one can enjoy the Israel Philharmonic Orchestra or any number of other musical or theatrical productions. And it is in Haifa that many of the country's technologically bright minds are educated.

The Bahai Shrine, located on Mount Carmel, is recognized as that faith's most important site and is visited annually by thousands of pilgrims.

Boasting a population of nearly five hundred thousand, Haifa stands as an example of the applied principles of productivity and prosperity, all of which are embodied in the Israeli work ethic.

Tel Aviv, noticeably more cosmopolitan and reflecting a Western influence, is a busy, beautiful city that almost seems out of place in such a historic land. Home to almost half a million people, the city has become the very hub of the country's business and industry. It is vibrant and alive with the young people who make up the lifeblood of Israel's future.

Only thirty-eight miles from Jerusalem, Tel Aviv/Jaffa dates back some six thousand years and boasts of archeological finds that validate its origins at some point between the Stone Age and the Bronze Age.

Tel Aviv exudes an aura of confidence in its ability to lead the country into the next century through an understanding of the necessity for the merging of the past, the present, and the future.

Education is a religious duty that Jews have always approached with joy. From biblical times, the study of the Jewish scriptures was considered an important commitment. Throughout the Diaspora, Jewish parents taught their children the laws and traditions in order to ensure the survival of their culture and religion. Today, Israel has undertaken the education of its diverse community members with its traditional energy and zeal.

A free, compulsory education is provided for all children up to age fifteen or through the eighth grade. After grade school, Israeli youth must choose between high school or work. High schools emphasize college preparatory, vocational, or religious curricula. Many students choose the vocational course of study, called "professional," in order to learn a trade immediately. This is a respected choice in Israel and does not carry the "blue collar" negative connotation prevalent in some Western countries. Other students attend a Secondary *Yeshiva,* a *Talmudic* academy that combines both secular and religious studies.

The majority of the grade school children attend state schools which range from the most conservative to the innovative. Approximately one-fifth of these students attend Jewish denominational schools. Until recently these were generally the most traditional schools, modeled after the Orthodox *Yeshiva,* or *Talmud* school. Now many non-Orthodox Israelis are

From sweets to sheepskins, olives to ointments, a variety of wares is displayed in shops in the Arab Quarter of the Old City.

The Kidron Valley separates Mount Moriah from the Mount of Olives.

choosing Jewish schools for what they perceive to be a more modern approach to Judaism. These schools are similar to the Conservative and Reform movements of Judaism in America.

In addition, almost one-fourth of the school-age children attend schools taught in Arabic. Many Arabs receive monetary assistance from the state for textbooks and scholarships to attend high school and college.

Israel places a priority on education for its many immigrants, providing intensive language instruction to enhance their adjustment to their new homeland. Grants have also been provided for a large part of the population which comes from underdeveloped countries, so educational differences are gradually being eliminated.

After high school, Jews, Druze, and Circassians must serve in the military. Moslems and Christians may volunteer, but for them, enlistment is not compulsory. Men serve for three years; women, for two. Upon release from the service, some return to their trades while others go to college.

Jerusalem, Tel Aviv, Haifa, Ramat Gan, and Beersheba all have universities. Two of those founded before statehood are the Hebrew University in Jerusalem, and the Technion — the Israel Institute of Technology — in Haifa. Others include Bar-Ilan, the Weizmann Institute for Science, the Bezalel School of Art and Drama, and the University of Tel Aviv.

Some students choose the traditional *yeshiva*. Here, young men immerse themselves in rabbinical study or as the first step in a lifetime of religious study, a highly respected way of life for Orthodox Jews. The *yeshivot* (plural of *yeshiva*), a vital part of Jewish life since ancient times, continue to be important to Israel's strong Orthodox community.

THE FUTURE

Only a land and a people profoundly blessed by God could have survived the torments of the past. While the Arabs, Christians, and Jews have often been divided, tension has come from *within* each group as well.

But this "test of metal" has become the very foundation on which this land and country is built. In essence, the very tension that challenged the land and its people has proved to be the fertile ground on which to grow a new Israel.

Where Israel is headed depends upon so many variables, but most religious and political leaders agree that improved understanding and tolerance are the only sound answers to a bright future. Problems that might appear totally insignificant elsewhere, in Israel, often yield international conflicts; thus, Israel always seems to be on the brink of another war or a new territorial dispute.

The obvious answer to all of this lies in the people — *all* of the people who make up the tapestry of modern-day Israel.

Islamic and Christian Arabs must open new doors to peaceful coexistence; likewise, the Jews *must* do the same. If Israel is to emerge as the Land of Promise, it must build its promise on the strength and stability that comes through mutual respect and cooperation. In that environment, everyone wins! Education becomes more vibrant as it is freed from the shackles of the past and allowed to open up the exciting new world of information and technology to everyone.

Similarly, religious leaders must work side-by-side to project peace. No matter where they come from philosophically or spiritually, this new effort of cooperation will further aid the stability of the land and dramatically reduce the "erosion" that results from conflict and bloodshed in the name of any faith or belief.

Culture, too, will be expanded once there is less fear and more trust and openness. While the performing and visual arts — coupled with designers of artisan crafts — contribute to an amazing patchwork of talent and skills, the country remains held back by division and mistrust. Once all these artistic resources pool their talents and develop an alliance of cultural inter-dependence, Israel will be farther along the way to a lasting peace.

Business and industry have taken an unusual path to their present state. Here, too, the burdens of past grievances have impeded progress. However, in cities like Tel Aviv, one finds an entrepreneurial atmosphere that must now filter into other regions. Certainly the enterprises of the *kibbutzim* have provided the initial spark — but now Israel's time to take its place in the international marketplace has come.

At no other time in her history has Israel so *needed* this new atmosphere of collective trust and cooperation. Truly, her time has come.

Israel's Jews, Christians, and Moslems must renew their commitment to working together in harmony, so that the very destiny of this land can be fulfilled — a land of promise!

> And He shall judge between the nations,
> And shall decide for many peoples;
> And they shall beat their swords into plowshares,
> And their spears into pruning-hooks;
> Nation shall not lift up sword against nation,
> Neither shall they learn war any more.

Isaiah 2:4

High above the Old City, the chapel of the Ethiopian Monastery is located on the roof of the Church of the Holy Sepulchre. The church is believed by many to be built on the hill called Golgotha, the site of Jesus' crucifixion, and over the tomb thought to have been used by Joseph of Arimathea for Jesus' burial.

■ *Above:* For over five hundred years, Ethiopian Abyssinian monks have made their home in a monastery and chapel located on the rooftop of the Church of the Holy Sepulchre. ■ *Right:* The Old City of Jerusalem is a maze of homes, shops, alleyways, rooftops, and present-day solar energy panels. Courtyards nestled inside the Old City offer privacy for its residents.

Persian tiles decorate an entrance to the Dome of the Rock Mosque. Each entrance is aligned with the points of the compass.

■ *Previous Page:* The Western Wall, or Wailing Wall, is the only remaining portion of the walls which once surrounded the Second Temple. Jews have prayed here for centuries, tucking prayers written on tiny slips of paper among the stones of the 2,000-year-old wall. ■ *Above:* King David ordered the construction of Jerusalem's first walls. His son, Solomon, known as the architect of the city, added lavish shrines and monuments within the walls.

The Western Wall is a popular place to gather for religious discussions as well as for prayer.

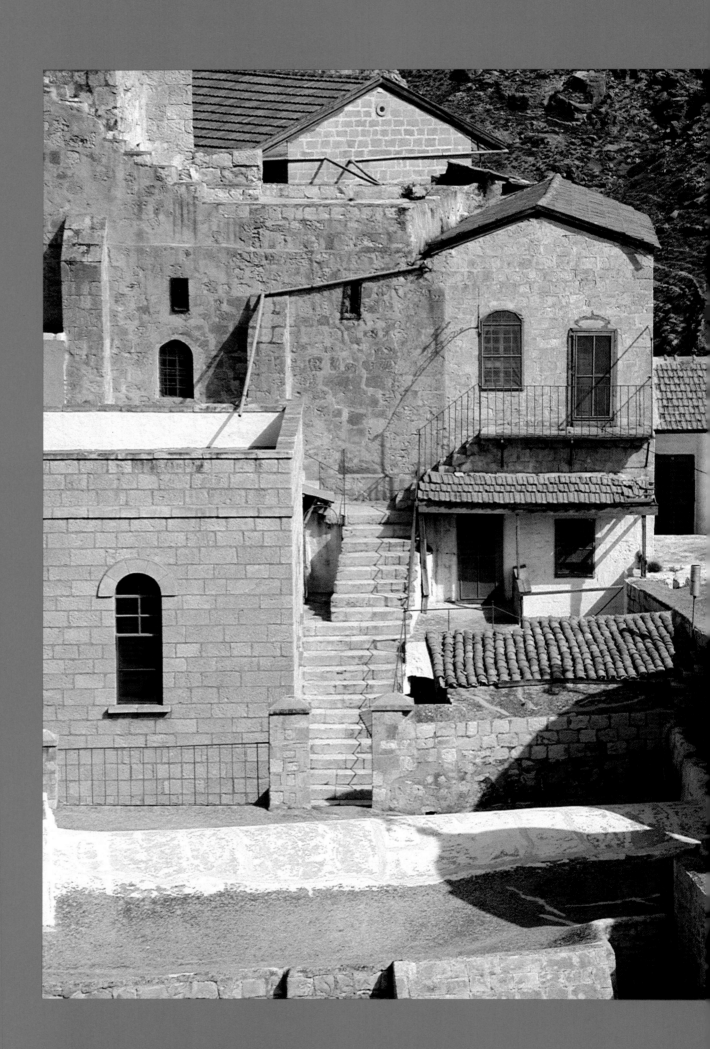

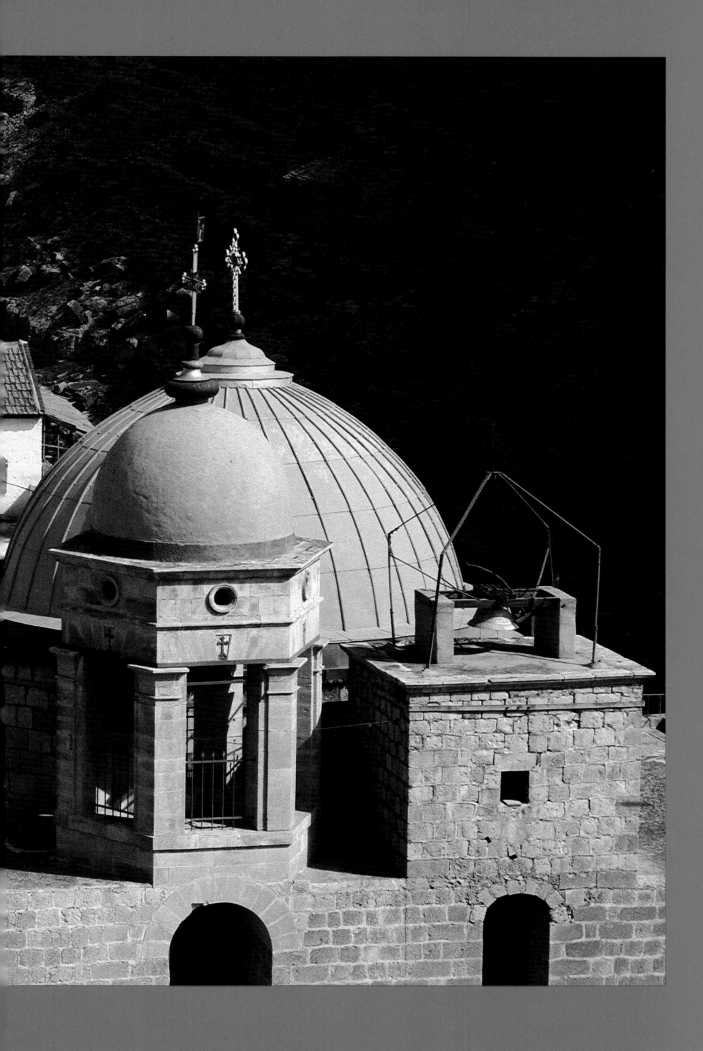

■ *Pages 40-41:* The Monastery of Mar Saba, constructed in the fifth century, was restored in the early 1800s by the Imperial Russian Government. ■ *Left:* Privacy is guarded in crowded Jerusalem, and courtyards or secluded areas are rare. ■ *Above:* A wailing vendor sells her wares inside St. Stephen's Gate, or Lions Gate, where Stephen, the first Christian martyr, is believed to have been stoned after his conviction by the Sanhedrin.

■ *Above:* Near Herodian and Bethlehem, travelers enter a land unchanged by the centuries. ■ *Right:* Seen from the roof of the Church of the Nativity, thought to be the site of the birth of Jesus, Bethlehem is a predominantly Arab town of commercial shops and apartments.

■ *Left:* The East Gate and wall of Old Jerusalem are seen from the arch of the Church of the Nations on the Mount of Olives. ■ *Above:* The evening lights expose the modern city of West Jerusalem filled with office buildings, public agencies, ministries, and parliamentary buildings. The city continues to expand northward as new residential areas are built.

Since ancient times, nomadic Bedouin tribes have wandered the Judean Desert, which lies along the mountains of Samaria, the Dead Sea, and the Jordan Valley. The isolation of the area makes it an ideal location for monasteries such as the nearby Monastery of Mar Saba. It is here that Jesus spent forty days and forty nights in meditation.

An Arab woman lives on the rooftop of the Church of the Nativity.

■ *Left:* Following an ancient custom, a rock is left behind to mark each visit by family and friends to a Jewish grave. This cemetery is located on the Mount of Olives and is one of many that are situated near the Old City. ■ *Above:* Orthodox Jews recite prayers at the grave of a loved one.

■ *Above:* East of Jerusalem one can see a dramatic view near Shepherd's Hills.
■ *Right:* These columns are part of the Ascension Chapel, located on the Mount of Olives, Jerusalem. The original chapel was built by the Crusaders in the twelfth century and was later occupied by the Moslems.

■ *Left:* The Damascus Gate, the most elaborate of the gates built by Suleiman the Magnificent in 1537, marks the ancient route from Jerusalem to Damascus. ■ *Above:* Camel bags, used since ancient times for carrying water, are no less important today in this land where water supplies continue to be a primary concern. ■ *Overleaf:* Rebuilt walls inside the Jewish Quarter of the Old City again provide sanctuary for area residents.

■ *Above:* The Dead Sea, from which salt, potash and other minerals are extracted, is the world's lowest point below sea level. Most scholars believe that Sodom and Gomorrah are buried at its southern end. ■ *Right:* The oasis of En Gedi, once a refuge for David, is known throughout the world today for its dates which are watered by natural springs and for a resort that is a popular stopping-place for travelers en route to the Dead Sea or Massada.

The canyon of Wadi Kelt is the site of the Monastery of St. George, near Jericho.

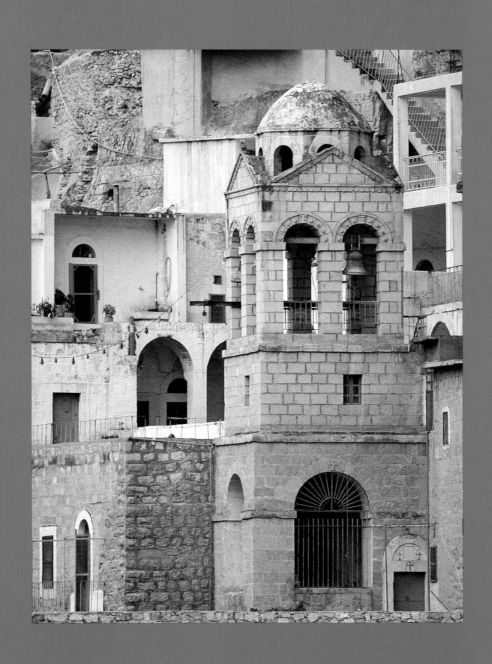

■ *Page 61:* A reminder of early Christians who fled to the rugged area to escape persecution, the Monastery of St. George, established in the fifth century, is located on the West Bank. ■ *Left:* Tel Arad, a Canaanite and Israelite excavation, dates back to the Bronze Age. ■ *Above:* Avdat, over two thousand years old, was founded by the Nabateans, a tribe from Arabia.

Precious water flows from picturesque En Avdat, now a protected area. The natural spring, one of the largest in the usually dry Negev, is located near Avdat, a popular tourist stop. Ancient Avdat, dating back to the third century B.C.E., is the site of ruins of a hilltop fortification and a temple.

Dramatic rock formations distinguish the landscape in the Timna Valley, north of Eilat.

■ *Left:* Sandstone arches, carved by thousands of years of erosion, are one of the many unique natural features that can be seen on the edge of the Arava Rift near the Timna Valley. ■ *Above:* Near Eilat, a mountain juts abruptly from the Arava Rift Valley by the Israeli-Jordanian border. Also nearby are the once-famous copper mines of the region.

▮ *Above:* An afternoon thunderstorm over Eilat, Israel's most southern point, is a rarity. Situated near the Red Sea, Eilat is a resort area, drawing both Israeli and foreign tourists. ■ *Right:* At Ashkelon, Crusader fortifications dating back to the twelfth century are a grim reminder of this Mediterranean area's history. Ashkelon, Herod's birthplace, was famous during his reign for the bathhouses he built, and remains a popular recreation area.

■ *Left:* At Ashkelon north of Gaza, this popular Mediterranean beach is one of the many recreational areas that cater to vacationers. ■ *Above:* These arches, located at Caesarea between Tel Aviv and Haifa, are all that remain of what was once an ancient Crusader castle. ■ *Overleaf:* The port city of Haifa, bordering the Mediterranean Sea, seems never to sleep. Haifa is home to the Bahai Shrine and is a busy metropolitan center of business and industry.

■ *Left:* Gilded by golden sunshine against rain clouds, the sky is washed by a multi-colored rainbow — a symbol of hope that a lasting peace will soon come to all the people of Israel. ■ *Above:* This Roman theater, constructed in the first century in Caesarea between Tel Aviv and Haifa as a center for entertainment, is still used for musical and theatrical productions.

■ *Above:* Only a few miles from Haifa is Akko, once a strategic port for all of Palestine. ■ *Right:* Dating from the days of the Canaanites, Akko was home to the Crusaders and also endured numerous occupations. Today, this industrialized area of almost forty thousand residents is a center for Israel's iron and steel industry as well as chemical, ceramic, and fishing enterprises.

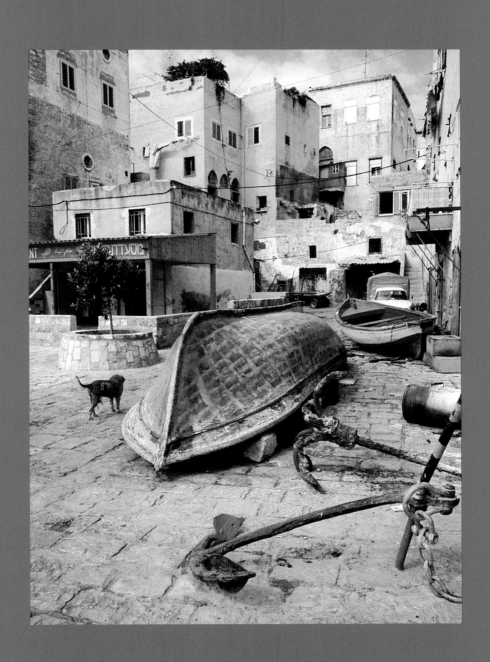

■ *Left:* Located near a mound of ruins which hold the buried secrets of yesterday, Akko is where St. Francis of Assisi established an order of nuns known as the Poor Clares in 1219. ■ *Above:* The Mediterranean shore at Rosh Hanikra is located on the Israeli-Lebanese border.

At Israel's most northwestern point are the sea grottoes of Rosh Hanikra, a natural phenomenon resulting from the waves pounding the shoreline cliffs. With no way to pass through or around them, ancient travelers were forced to climb the white chalk cliffs in order to go north to the Phoenician city of Tyre. Even today, the ascent still bears the name, the *Ladder of Tyre*.

The Montfort Fortress, constructed in the twelfth century, is located in the Upper Galilee in northern Israel.

■ *Left:* Safed, at 2,739 feet elevation, is the highest town in Israel and dates back to the first century. Located north of the Sea of Galilee, the community has a long history of conflict and has been occupied by many conquering forces. ■ *Above:* A fiery sunset illumines the sky over the hills of Galilee, the area where many of the events of the life of Jesus took place.

■ *Above:* Kibbutzim laborers have transformed the Hula Valley into a show-place of agricultural achievement. Fruits such as peaches, apples, and pears, as well as grains and peanuts, are grown in the area situated on the Lebanese border. ■ *Right:* A ram's horn and menorah are clearly visible in this remnant of a Capernaum synagogue dating back to the second or third century.

■ *Above:* For nearly twenty years, the Golan Heights was a Syrian army camp. It was captured by Israel during the Six-Day War in June of 1967. ■ *Right:* Nimrod's Castle was built by the Crusaders in the twelfth century as a fortress on the route from Damascus to Lebanon and the Mediterranean. ■ *Following Page:* Near Bet She'an, a decorative column dating back to approximately the second century, is a relic of the ornate Roman theaters.

■ *Left:* On the Sea of Galilee, a paradise for water sports enthusiasts, a wind surfer is wafted along by the breezes of a summer afternoon. It was here that Jesus and his disciples toiled in their fishing boats. ■ *Above:* Gamla, established during the period of the Second Temple, was destroyed by the Romans in 67 A.D. Located in the Golan, Gamla is now known for its memorial honoring Israelis who died in the 1973 Yom Kippur War.

■ *Above:* Reputed for its hot springs, Tiberias is a popular vacation spot. The city, founded in 17 A.D. by Herod Antipas, was named for Tiberias, the Emperor of Rome. ■ *Right:* The Sea of Galilee, whose tranquillity is often shattered by sudden and violent storms, is actually a lake rather than a sea.

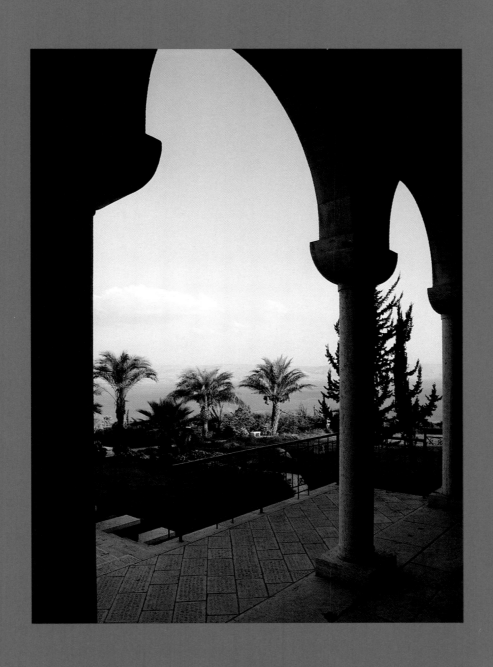

■ *Left:* The garden at the Mount of Beatitudes, believed by many to be the area where Jesus delivered the Sermon on the Mount, is covered year-round with lush greenery. ■ *Above:* The domed Church of the Beatitudes, built in 1937, is a unique eight-sided structure, each side signifying one of the Beatitudes. Jesus was said to have done much of his teaching in the area around Galilee.

Well-known for its biblical significance, the Jordan River is fed by numerous springs and ultimately winds its way to the Dead Sea. It was at the point where the Yarmuk, the largest of the tributaries, joins the Jordan River that the Arab armies won Palestine and Syria from the Byzantine Empire in 636 A.D., thus beginning the period of Islamic rule. Today, the broad and fertile floodplain of the Jordan River is the site of many agricultural villages.

Mount Tabor, mentioned in both the Old and the New Testaments, offers a view of the Arab village of Dabburiya. Residents of such rural communities have lived through many changes since Israel's independence in 1948. Compulsory education, equal rights for women, and modern agricultural technology have brought about social change and, at the same time, have raised the standard of living in these once-traditional Moslem towns.

■ *Above:* Strategically located in the Jordan valley, Belvoir was a Crusader castle built in the twelfth century. Belvoir, meaning "beautiful view," has also had a place in modern history. It was here that the Iraqi army turned back and fled across the Jordan River during the War of Independence. ■ *Right:* This *Sabra,* a citizen of birth, shares enthusiasm for her homeland.

Crowds mounted the worn steps of a Roman theater, erected at Bet She'an around 200 A.D., to view sporting events.

■ *Preceding Page:* The sun reflects off the mountains north of Massada, exposing the same barren terrain which must have greeted the Romans as they marched eastward to capture the Herodian fortress. ■ *Above:* Nazareth, the boyhood home of Jesus, is now the largest town in the Arab part of Israel. Its entirely Arab population of fifty thousand is composed half of Moslems and half of approximately twelve Christian denominations.

■ *Above:* A sculptor's studio in a deserted mosque is similar to the many studios found in the Artists' Quarter of Old Jaffa. Artisans of all disciplines make their homes in this area of Tel Aviv. ■ *Overleaf:* The Old Jaffa Port, situated on the Mediterranean, boasts a colorful history. The port witnessed the immigration of European Jews before 1900 and the influx of Western European Jews during and after the turmoil of World War II.

■ *Left:* Amid the studios and shops of Old Jaffa, this passageway leads to the old Armenian convent which once served as a hospital for Napoleon's troops. ■ *Above:* Everywhere in the world, a sweet shop is an enticement to weary tourists. In Old Jaffa, this bakery is located among many other shops, boutiques, studios, and cafés which line the intricate maze of narrow streets.

■ *Above:* Bicycles are common transportation in large cities such as Tel Aviv. Not only are they inexpensive to purchase and maintain, but they allow the owner to weave through heavy traffic without the usual rush-hour problems. This handpainted doorway and window reflect the work of an artist living in Old Jaffa. ■ *Right:* Fishing is still a major source of income, and boats docked at the Old Jaffa Port bring in their daily catches.

Today, Tel Aviv is a bustling metropolis which has joined hands with Jaffa to form a thriving community of well over one million. While Jerusalem is considered Israel's capital, all foreign embassies are located in Tel Aviv, which is also the country's industrial, commercial, and financial center. Free enterprise flourishes here, with many elegant boutiques and quality shops.

Area residents find tranquillity in public parks away from the city's hectic pace. Passing the time is easy in Tel Aviv, where there are many tourist attractions such as museums, cultural events, and sporting activities. Although most of the urban area consists of modern concrete buildings, there are parks, historical sites, and interesting architecture throughout the city.

"In the beginning God created the heaven and the earth . . . and darkness was upon the face of the deep; and the spirit of God hovered over the face of the waters. . . . And God said: 'Let the waters under the heaven be gathered together unto one place, and let the dry land appear,' and it was so. And God called the dry land Earth, and the gathering together of the waters He called Seas; and God saw that it was good." Genesis 1:1-2; 9-10